Saunders Book Club 99⁸26.00   J 629.132 mel

FLIGHT

PETER MELLETT

Gareth Stevens Publishing
MILWAUKEE

The original publishers would like to thank the following children, and their parents, for modeling in this book — Emily Askew, Sara Barnes, Maria Bloodworth, David Callega, Aaron Dumetz, Laurence de Freitas, Alistair Fulton, Anton Goldbourne, Sasha Howarth, Jon Leming, Jessica Moxley, Ifunanya Obi, Emily Preddie, Elen Rhys, Nicola Twiner, and Joe Westbrook.

Gareth Stevens Publishing would like to thank Kenneth Mischka for his assistance with the accuracy of the text. Mr. Mischka is Chair of the Aviation Maintenance Technician program at Milwaukee Area Technical College, Milwaukee, Wisconsin, where he also teaches courses in physics and electronics.

**For a free color catalog describing Gareth Stevens'
list of high-quality books and multimedia programs,
call 1-800-542-2595 (USA) or 1-800-461-9120 (Canada).
Gareth Stevens Publishing's Fax: (414) 225-0377.
See our catalog, too, on the World Wide Web: http://gsinc.com**

Library of Congress Cataloging-in-Publication Data

Mellett, P. (Peter), 1946-
Flight / by Peter Mellett.
p. cm. — (Young scientist concepts and projects)
Includes bibliographical references and index.
Summary: Explains the concepts of flight and aeronautics while also suggesting experiments which further illustrate the information presented.
ISBN 0-8368-2162-9 (lib. bdg.)
1. Flight—Juvenile literature. 2. Aeronautics—Juvenile literature.
[1. Flight—Experiments. 2. Aeronautics—Experiments.
3. Experiments.] I. Title. II. Series.
TL547.M46   1998
629.132—dc21   98-4841

This North American edition first published in 1998 by
Gareth Stevens Publishing
1555 North RiverCenter Drive, Suite 201
Milwaukee, WI 53212 USA

Original edition © 1997 by Anness Publishing Limited.
First published in 1997 by Lorenz Books, an imprint of
Anness Publishing Inc., New York, New York.
This U.S. edition © 1998 by Gareth Stevens, Inc.
Additional end matter © 1998 by Gareth Stevens, Inc.

Editor: Charlotte Evans
Consultant: Chris Oxlade
Photographer: John Freeman
Stylists: Marion Elliot and Melanie Williams
Designer: Caroline Grimshaw
Picture researcher: Liz Eddison
Illustrator: Dave Bowyer
Gareth Stevens series editor: Dorothy L. Gibbs
Editorial assistant: Diane Laska

Printed in the United States of America

1 2 3 4 5 6 7 8 9 02 01 00 99 98

FLIGHT

CONTENTS

WHAT IS FLIGHT?

THINK of flight and you think: birds and insects, airplanes and helicopters, arrows and footballs. All of these things can move swiftly through the air, but are they all actually flying? To answer this question, imagine that you are throwing a paper airplane. It glides away from you and, finally, lands back on the ground. If you throw a football exactly the same way, it hits the ground much sooner than the paper airplane. The paper airplane was flying; the football was not, because footballs, stones, and arrows all are projectiles. They do not actually fly because they have nothing to keep them up in the air. Birds, airplanes, rockets, and balloons *do* fly — they stay off the ground longer than something that is simply thrown.

Animal power
Birds, insects, and bats all have wings. They use their wings to hold themselves up in the air and to fly forward. Their muscles provide power for takeoff.

Balloons
This balloon is filled with a gas called helium. Helium is lighter than air, so the balloon floats upward, like a cork floats upward in water. Before airplanes and rockets were invented, the only way anyone could make a sustained flight was in a craft that was lighter than air, such as a hot-air balloon.

Spaceflight
A space shuttle is launched into space by powerful booster rockets. It uses its own rocket engines to reach an orbit about 180 miles (290 kilometers) above Earth. Earth's gravity acts like a tether, keeping the shuttle in orbit. The shuttle's speed prevents it from falling back to the ground.

Airplanes

Like birds, airplanes have wings to hold them up in the air, but airplanes also have engines. Engine power is needed to help them take off from the ground and to push them through the air.

Tether

Flying a kite

A blowing wind lifts a kite into the air. A long string, called a tether, holds the kite at an angle to the wind. Rushing air pushes against the kite, forcing it upward and keeping it in the air. If the wind dies down or the tether breaks, the kite will fall back to the ground.

Gliders

Gliders have no engines. They have to be towed into the air by small airplanes or by machines on the ground. When released from the tow, their wings hold them up in the air as they glide slowly to the ground in a gentle spiral. A pilot controls a glider's flight by searching for rising air currents and by altering the shape of the glider's wings.

WINGS AND LIFT

FLAP your arms up and down like a bird — you cannot take off because you are not designed to fly. You are the wrong shape, and your muscles are not strong enough. A bird has wings and powerful muscles that enable it to fly. Flapping its wings provides a force, called thrust, that moves the bird forward through the air. A bird's wing is an airfoil, which has a special shape; the top side is more curved than underneath. This shape helps keep the bird up in the air, even when its wings are not flapping. When airfoil wings move through the air, they create an upward push, called lift. Lift works against the weight of the flying object which, because of gravity, is pulling that object down toward the ground. Birds, gliders, and airplanes come in many different shapes and sizes, but they all have airfoil wings.

Blowing across a sheet of paper reduces the pressure of the air above the paper. Stronger air pressure underneath lifts the paper up.

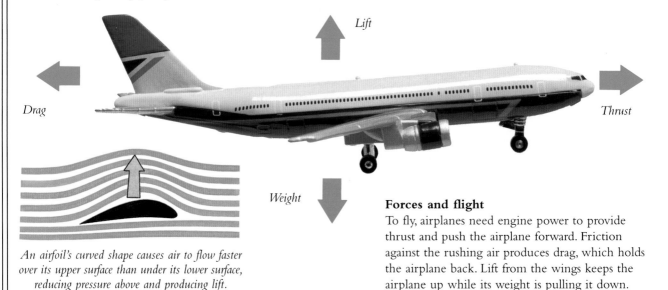

Lift

Drag

Thrust

Weight

An airfoil's curved shape causes air to flow faster over its upper surface than under its lower surface, reducing pressure above and producing lift.

Forces and flight
To fly, airplanes need engine power to provide thrust and push the airplane forward. Friction against the rushing air produces drag, which holds the airplane back. Lift from the wings keeps the airplane up while its weight is pulling it down.

Wings and soaring

This bird is soaring through the air without flapping its wings. Its wings slice through the air creating lift, which pushes up on them. The faster the bird's speed, the greater the lift. Some birds can soar for hours.

FACT BOX

• A Boeing 747-400 weighs about 400 tons (363 metric tons) at takeoff. A third of this weight is fuel, which is stored in the aircraft's wings. This jumbo jet has a wingspan of 211 feet (64.3 meters).

• The speed of a jumbo jet reaches almost 180 miles (290 km) per hour at takeoff.

• Most helicopters have three to six rotor blades. Some blades are over 30 feet (9 m) long, but only about 1½ feet (0.5 m) wide.

• Half the weight of a pigeon is taken up by the flight muscles needed to flap its wings.

• A boomerang is a bent airfoil wing. One of the oldest boomerangs — about 20,000 years old — was found in a cave in Poland.

Helicopters

Airplanes have airfoil wings that do not move. Planes must rush through the air to help their wings produce lift. Helicopters have long, thin airfoil wings, called rotor blades. Powerful engines whirl these blades around to produce lift. Helicopters can hover or fly forward, backward, or sideways, as well as straight up and down.

Taking off

Most airplanes need long runways to take off. They speed along, going faster and faster, until the lift pushing up is greater than the weight pulling down, which allows them to leave the ground.

MAKE AN AIRFOIL

BIRDS, gliders, and airplanes all have wings. Their wings might be different shapes and sizes, but they all have the same airfoil design — the top side of the wing is more curved than underneath. Whether on a tiny sparrow or a huge airplane, an airfoil provides lift as air moves over it. Air flows faster over the curved upper surface than under the flatter, lower surface, reducing air pressure above the wing and allowing stronger air pressure underneath to lift it up. The projects on these two pages explain how to make and test model airfoils that show you how moving air lifts wings upward. In the first project, you can make a throwing disk, a circular airfoil shaped like a dish. Like a straight-wing airfoil, air flows faster over the disk's top surface than underneath. As the disk flies, its spinning motion helps keep it steady.

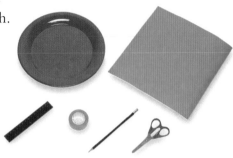

M A T E R I A L S

You will need:
a large plastic plate, thick cardboard,
pencil, scissors, ruler, tape.

Make a throwing disk

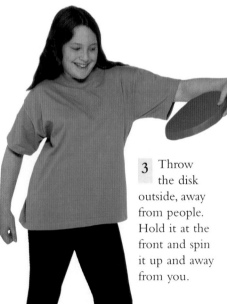

1 Use a plate (facedown) to draw a circle on cardboard. Cut out the circle. Draw lines about 1 inch (2.5 centimeters) deep all around the edge *(as shown)*. Cut along the lines.

2 These cuts will create tabs around the edge of the circle. Bend the tabs toward you slightly, overlapping them a little, and tape them together.

3 Throw the disk outside, away from people. Hold it at the front and spin it up and away from you.

Make an airfoil

1 On paper, draw a 6- x 8-inch (15- x 20-cm) rectangle with a line across the middle. Cut it out.

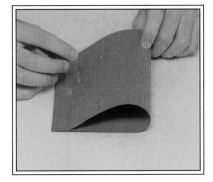

2 Fold the paper over and tape down one edge about ½ inch (1.2 cm) away from the other edge.

3 Cut out a small paper fin and tape it to the flat edge of the "wing" to keep the wing facing into the airflow when you test it.

MATERIALS

You will need: paper, sharp pencil, ruler, scissors, tape, plastic drinking straw, glue, thick cotton yarn.

4 With a sharp pencil, poke holes through the top and bottom of the wing, near the folded edge. Push a straw through both holes and glue it in place at the middle.

5 Cut a piece of yarn 3 feet (1 m) long and thread it through the straw. Make sure the yarn slides easily through the straw and does not catch.

To test the airfoil, hold the yarn tightly and let air from a fan or hair dryer blow over the wing. Watch it take off!

AIR RESISTANCE

WHEN you swim, you have to push your way through the water. The water resists you and slows you down. In the same way, things that fly have to push their way through the air. Air clings to their surfaces as they rush through it, causing a backward pull, called drag or air resistance, that works against the direction of flight. Drag is the force that slows down anything flying through the air. The amount of drag is determined by shape. Fat, lumpy shapes with sharp edges create a lot of drag. They disturb the air and make it swirl around as they move along. Sleek, streamlined shapes have low drag and can fly the fastest. They disturb the air very little as they cut smoothly through it. For any shape, increasing the speed increases the drag. Doubling the speed creates four times the amount of drag. Clearly, drag limits how fast anything can fly.

Parachutes are designed to have very high drag. They fall slowly because they trap air underneath.

Angle of attack

When an aircraft is in flight, the angle of its wings against the flow of air is called the angle of attack. As the angle of attack increases, the amount of lift also increases.

If the angle of attack increases too much, lift drops suddenly, because the smooth flow of air over the wing is broken, creating turbulence, increasing drag, and reducing lift.

Turbulence

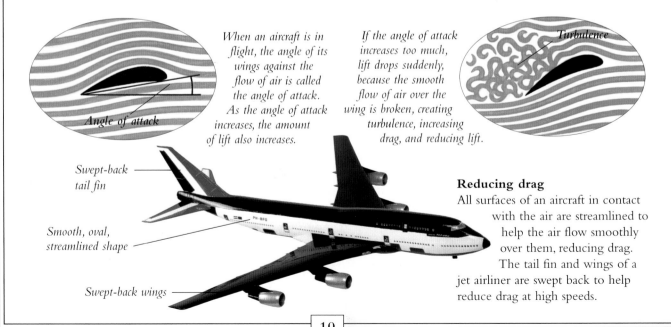

Swept-back tail fin

Smooth, oval, streamlined shape

Swept-back wings

Reducing drag

All surfaces of an aircraft in contact with the air are streamlined to help the air flow smoothly over them, reducing drag. The tail fin and wings of a jet airliner are swept back to help reduce drag at high speeds.

Birds must slow down before they land. An owl tips up its wings so the undersides face forward. It also lowers and spreads out its tail feathers to act as a brake. Drag increases suddenly, lift decreases, and the bird descends to its landing place.

The Lockheed SR-71 lands at 210 miles (338 km) per hour. A parachute helps slow it down, because using only ordinary brakes on its wheels would take too long.

The Concorde can fly at speeds of over 1,200 miles (1,900 km) per hour. Its wings are swept back to reduce drag. If its wings stuck straight out, they would be ripped off at such high speeds.

Coming in to land, this airliner is using the flaps on its wings to increase lift at lower speeds. During flight, these flaps are retracted to reduce drag.

STREAMLINING AND SHAPE

Tнink of a sleek canoe moving through water. Its streamlined shape causes very few ripples. Streamlined shapes also move easily through air because they have low drag. Drag, also called air resistance, is the force that works against the forward motion of flight. The amount of drag is determined by shape. Angular shapes create more drag than rounded ones. Design and test your own shapes, or make a model parachute to find out how its shape creates high drag so it will fall slowly.

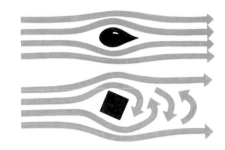

Air flows smoothly around the streamlined shape (top). Angles and sharp edges break up the air flow (bottom) and increase drag.

Shape race
Use modeling clay to make different shapes (*as shown at the right*) that are all the same size. Race your shapes in water. The most streamlined shape should reach the bottom first.

Star shape   *Square shape*   *Teardrop shape*

How much of a splash would you make diving into a pool? This diver's streamlined shape will help her cut cleanly through the water to dive down deep.

MATERIALS

You will need:
a large plate, thin fabric,
felt-tip pen, scissors,
cotton thread, needle, tape,
plastic thread spool.

Make a parachute

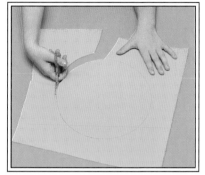

1 With the plate facedown on the fabric, draw around it with a felt-tip pen. Cut out the circle for the parachute's canopy.

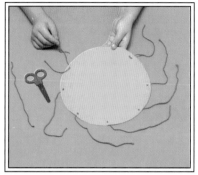

2 Make 8 marks equally spaced around the edge of the circle. Cut 8 pieces of thread 12 inches (30 cm) long. Use a needle to sew on a piece of thread at each mark.

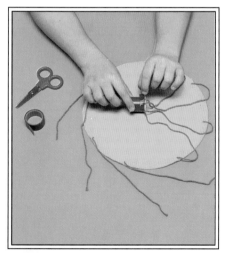

3 Tape the free end of each piece of thread to the spool. Be sure to use a plastic spool, because a wooden one will be too heavy for the parachute.

4 Drop the parachute from as high up as possible. As it falls, the canopy will open and fill with air. The larger the canopy, the slower the parachute will fall.

GLIDING AND SOARING

A glider's long, thin wings provide maximum lift and minimum drag for their size. If a glider flies level in still air, drag slows it down, and its wings lose their lift. So, to keep its speed up, a glider flies on a gradual downward slope.

WATCH a small bird fly. It flaps its little wings very fast almost the entire time. Large birds, however, can glide with their wings stretched out flat and still, because their large wings create enough lift to keep them up in the air without flapping. Soaring birds, such as albatrosses and condors, fly for hours, hardly moving their wings at all. They fly upward over land and sea using rising air currents. Gliders are aircraft without engines that have wings like those of soaring birds. They must be pulled along, or towed, by small aircraft or machines on the ground until the lift generated by their wings keeps them airborne. Glider pilots look for rising air currents, called thermals, to lift their aircraft upward.

Going up

To fly upward, glider pilots look for rising air currents, or thermals. Thermals occur where the wind is forced upward by cliffs or hillsides, or where the air is heated by the ground. Hot air rises because it is pushed up by the colder air around it. The pilot circles the glider inside the thermal, steadily gaining height as the rising air carries it upward. At the top of the thermal, where the effect is weaker, the pilot stops circling.

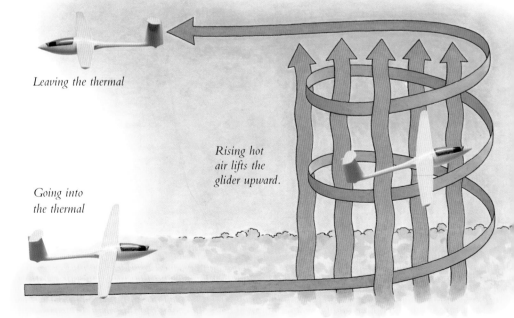

Leaving the thermal

Going into the thermal

Rising hot air lifts the glider upward.

Paragliders

Air blowing into pockets along the front edge of a paraglider's wing creates its aerodynamic shape. The pilot steers from side to side and can ride up thermals.

An albatross has the longest wingspan of any bird, over 9 feet (3 m) long. The long, narrow shape of its wings helps it glide for incredible distances on air currents blowing over the open ocean.

Inside a glider's cockpit (above), the dial on the left shows forward air speed, the dial in the middle shows how fast the glider is going up (climbing) or down (descending), and the dial on the right shows how high the glider is above ground (altitude).

Hang gliders

A hang glider is very light. Its wing is made of strong, thin material on a framework of aluminum poles. The material is stretched into an airfoil shape to produce lift. To steer a hang glider, the pilot moves a control bar forward to climb and backward to dive.

KITES

Have you ever been blown over by the wind? Wind is moving air — it pushes against anything in its path. A kite flies because the force of the wind pushing against it holds it up in the air. A string, called a tether, keeps the kite connected to something or someone on the ground and holds it at the correct angle to the wind. The tension you feel along the tether as it pulls on your hand is the result of the wind blowing against the kite and lifting it up. If the tether breaks, the kite will no longer be at the correct angle to the wind, and it will fall to the ground. When there is no wind, you can still fly a kite by pulling it through the air.

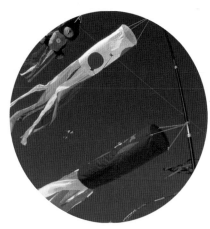

Windsock kites have open "mouths" to catch the wind. Like all kites, they will fly only when the wind blows against them.

Lift
Air blowing against the kite creates lift.

Flying a kite

What makes a kite fly? Wind is deflected downward when it blows against a kite, pushing the kite upward and creating lift and drag. The tether keeps the kite at an angle to the wind (the angle of attack). In a good breeze, a kite's weight is small compared to the forces of lift and drag.

Drag
Air moving over and around the kite causes drag.

Weight
The kite's weight pulls it down toward the ground.

Pull on tether
The tether holds the kite at an angle to the wind.

Flat kites

The oldest and simplest kite is the plane surface, or flat, kite. It has a simple diamond shape and a flat frame. Kites like these have been flown for thousands of years. Flat kites strung together *(left)* make a spectacular, writhing pattern in the sky.

FACT BOX

• The first kites were made in China over 3,000 years ago. Seven hundred years ago, kites were used to lift people into the sky to spy on enemy armies.

• In 1901, the first radio message was sent across the Atlantic Ocean. It was received by a 360-foot (110-m) aerial held up by a kite.

• Some kites carry weather forecasting instruments nearly 5 miles (8 km) high — almost as high as Mount Everest.

Box kites

A square-shaped box kite is more complicated to make than a flat kite, but it is more stable and has better lift. It does not need a tail to keep it upright. Box kites can be a combination of triangles and rectangles. Large box kites have been used even to lift people off the ground.

Parasails

A parasail is a kite that can lift a person into the air. It does not rely on the wind but, instead, is towed behind a boat or a car. A parasail looks like a parachute that has been divided into sections, called cells. Each cell works independently, catching as much wind as possible to provide lift. Parasails usually fly about 150 feet (45 m) above the ground.

MAKE A KITE

OR 3,000 years, people have been making and
flying kites. The first kites were made from
cloth or paper attached to a light bamboo frame.
As time went by, the simple secret to building a
good kite was discovered — make it as light as
possible for its size. Some kites can fly in very
gentle breezes. Their surfaces are wide so the breeze
has a large area to push against. Their light
weight needs only a small amount of lift to
make them take off into the sky. The flat kite
you can make in this project is a basic design that
has been used for hundreds of years. Fly this kite in
a steady wind. You might have to experiment with
the position of the bridle and the length of the tail.

*This kite's long tail
will help keep the kite
under control, so it
doesn't spin around.*

Make a kite

1 To make the kite's frame, mark
the center of the short stick
of wood and one-third of the way
down the long stick. Tie the wood
together with string at these marks.

2 Run more string around the
frame, taping it to the ends of
each stick of wood and securing
both ends of the string at the top
of the frame.

3 Lay the frame on the sheet of
fabric or plastic. Cut all around
it, 1½ inches (3.7 cm) away from the
string to leave enough material to
fold over the string outline.

4 Fold the edges of the material over the frame and glue them down firmly. Let the glue dry completely. (If you are making the kite from plastic, use tape to secure the edges.)

5 Tie a piece of string to the long piece of the frame *(as shown)*. This string is called the bridle. Tie the end of a ball of string to the middle of the bridle for a tether.

6 To make a tail, fold squares of colored paper accordion-style. Tie them about every 10 inches (25 cm) along a piece of string that is twice as long as the kite. Tie or glue the tail to the bottom tip of the kite.

This kite was designed to look like a face with a long trailing mustache. Decorative patterns can make even the simplest kite look very special. Have fun experimenting with the basic kite shown in this project.

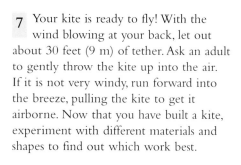

7 Your kite is ready to fly! With the wind blowing at your back, let out about 30 feet (9 m) of tether. Ask an adult to gently throw the kite up into the air. If it is not very windy, run forward into the breeze, pulling the kite to get it airborne. Now that you have built a kite, experiment with different materials and shapes to find out which work best.

LIGHTER THAN AIR

OIL floats on water because it is lighter, or less dense, than water. A bottle full of oil, then, weighs less than the same bottle full of water. When oil and water are put together, the water pushes upward on the oil with a force called upthrust. Similarly, hot air is less dense than the cold air around it. When smoke rises from a fire, it is because the hot air is pushed upward, taking the smoke with it. A hot-air balloon is simply a huge bag full of hot air. The balloon takes off because upthrust from the cold air around it is greater than its own weight pulling it down. Airships, like balloons, also are lighter than the air around them. Modern airships are filled with a gas called helium, which is seven times lighter than air. Hot-air balloons and airships fly because the air around them pushes them upward —
just like oil on water.

A candle heats the air around it. When you blow out the flame, the rising hot air will carry the smoke upward.

Oil and water
Oil floats on water because it is less dense than water. The water surrounding the oil pushes upward on it. This push is called upthrust.

FACT BOX

• The very first balloon passengers were a sheep, a duck, and a bird. They were sent up to make sure it was safe for people to travel in this new form of transport.

• The first balloon flight was over Paris on November 21, 1783. It lasted 25 minutes.

• The first airship flight was in France in 1852. Engineer Henri Giffard flew a steam-driven aircraft about 18 miles (29 km) at an average speed of 5 miles (8 km) per hour.

• The world's largest airship, the German *Hindenburg,* was 750 feet (229 m) long. It was destroyed by fire in 1937 when it crashed on landing, killing 35 people.

The first aviators
In 1783, brothers Joseph and Jacques Montgolfier built an enormous paper balloon and lit a fire underneath it. The balloon floated into the sky, safely carrying two people on the first journey by hot-air balloon.

Hot-air balloons
Modern hot-air balloons are made of nylon and are twice as tall as a house. They can carry about five people in a basket hanging underneath. All hot-air balloons can go only where the wind blows them.

Modern airships
Today's airships use helium to float and have engines and propellers to drive them along. A pilot steers this kind of airship by moving the fins on its tail.

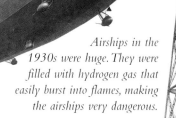

Airships in the 1930s were huge. They were filled with hydrogen gas that easily burst into flames, making the airships very dangerous.

MAKE A HOT-AIR BALLOON

Hot-air balloons rise into the sky because the hot air inside them is lighter than the cold air around them. As air heated by gas burners fills the main part of the balloon, called the envelope, the hot air pushes the cold air out of the way. The envelope holds about 2½ tons (2.3 metric tons) of hot air, approximately the same weight as two cars. The weight of the cold air is about 3½ tons (3.2 metric tons). The resulting upthrust is enough to lift the balloon, its passengers, and its tanks of gas off the ground. The project on the next page shows you how to make and fly your own hot-air balloon.

You will need:
cardboard, pencil, ruler, scissors, 7 pieces
of tissue paper, glue stick, hair dryer.

Stabilize a balloon
Attach some modeling clay to the string of a helium balloon. Add clay until the downward force (weight) equals the upward force (upthrust) and the balloon hangs steady.

Gas burners
Roaring gas burners heat the air inside this balloon. It takes more than half an hour to fill the balloon's envelope. When the envelope is full, the balloon is launched by untying the ropes that hold it to the ground.

Make a hot-air balloon

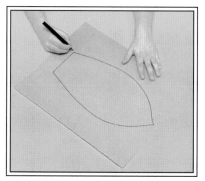

1 On cardboard, draw a petal-shaped pattern, 12 inches (30 cm) long and 5 inches (12.5 cm) across. Cut out the pattern.

2 Draw around the pattern onto the pieces of tissue paper. Be careful not to rip the tissue with the tip of your pencil.

3 Cut out the shapes you have drawn. You should have seven tissue paper petals that are all the same size and shape.

4 Glue along one edge of a petal. Press another petal on top of it. Open these two petals and keep gluing on and opening petals this way until the balloon is complete.

5 To make the balloon fly, hold its neck open and fill the inside with hot air from a hair dryer. After ten seconds, turn off the hair dryer and let go of the balloon to launch it into the air.

WARNING
Some hairdryers can get hot enough to start paper on fire.

BIRDS IN FLIGHT

MUSCLE-POWERED flight is very hard work. Although some have tried, no human has ever flown by flapping artificial wings. Compared to humans, birds are light and very powerful. They are perfectly designed to stay up in the air. Birds' wings are covered with feathers — one of the strongest and lightest natural materials known. The airfoil shape of their wings provides lift, and tail feathers help with steering and braking. Birds flap their wings hard to take off and climb into the air. A bird needs enormous flight muscles to provide enough power to fly. These muscles can account for up to half of the bird's weight and are supplied with blood pumped by a large heart beating very fast. To fly, a human would need a chest the size of a barrel, arms 9 feet (2.7 m) long, legs like broom handles, and a head the size of an apple — not to mention thousands of feathers!

Barb

Microscopic hooks lock each barb together so that air cannot pass through a feather.

Primary feathers

Flight feathers
The large primary feathers on the end of each wing produce most of a bird's power for flight. These feathers also can be spread apart or closed together to control flight. Smaller secondary feathers on the inner wing form the curve that provides lift. The innermost feathers shape the wing into the bird's body and help prevent turbulence in flight.

Secondary feathers

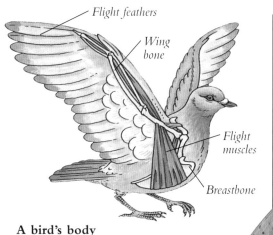

Flight feathers
Wing bone
Flight muscles
Breastbone

A bird's body

A bird's bones are light; most are hollow and filled with air. Flight feathers are connected to thin bones at the end of each wing. The large flight muscles are anchored to the breastbone at the front of a bird's chest.

On the wing

This picture *(above)* shows how a bird flies. Its wings bend in the middle as they move upward. The feathers open to let air pass through the wings. On the powerful downstroke, the primary flight feathers slice through the air, pushing the air down and back and pulling the bird upward and forward.

FACT BOX

• A sparrow's heart beats 800 times a minute. When working very hard, a human heart beats only about 120 times a minute.

• Birds are the only animals covered with feathers. A large bird, such as a swan, has about 25,000 feathers, while a tiny hummingbird has only 1,000.

• Arctic terns migrate each year from the Arctic to the Antarctic and back again — a round trip of about 6,000 miles (9,650 km).

• The world's largest bird, the ostrich, is too heavy to fly. The world's largest flying bird, the Australian Kori bustard, weighs no more than about 40 pounds (18 kilograms).

Peregrine falcons are the fastest animals in the world. They fold back their wings to reduce drag and dive for prey at 210 miles (338 km) per hour. The force of the impact breaks the victim's neck.

HOW BIRDS FLY

Look at a large bird, such as a goose, flying through the sky. Can you describe how its wings are moving? Flying birds do not simply flap their wings up and down. Their wings are not stiff and flat. Each wing has a joint like an elbow in the middle. This joint allows the wing to bend on the upstroke and flatten on the downstroke. Birds also open and close their flight feathers. On the upstroke, the feathers are spread apart to let air pass easily through the wings. On the downstroke, the feathers are held together to provide the maximum amount of lift. Start the project on these two pages with a simple water test to feel how a bird's primary flight feathers work. Then make a model bird to see how birds move their wings in flight.

When a bird raises its wings (the upstroke), its flight feathers open to let air through. You can feel the effect by moving your hand through water with your fingers spread apart.

During the downstroke, a bird closes its flight feathers so its wings push hard against the air forcing the bird upward and forward. Close your fingers as you move your hand through water. Do you feel a difference?

Make a model bird

1 To make the bird's legs, fold a piece of paper in half lengthwise, several times, until it is about 1 inch (2.5 cm) across.

2 Fold this strip in half and make another fold at each end to form feet. Tape the feet to your work surface to keep the model stable.

3 To make the bird's body, roll a piece of paper into a tube and tape down the edge. Then tape the body to the legs.

4 To make wings, fold a piece of paper lengthwise into a strip about six times longer than it is wide. Fold the strip into a *W* shape.

5 Tape the wings onto the body. You now have a model bird. To see how a bird flies, hold one wing tip in each hand.

6 Move your hands in circles — one going clockwise, the other counterclockwise. At takeoff, a bird's wings make large, round circles.

MATERIALS

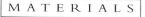
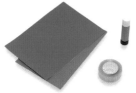

*You will need:
3 sheets of paper,
tape, glue stick.*

8 During the downstroke, notice how the wings become flatter. To see how a bird's wings move when the bird is flying level, move your hands far apart in small, flat circles.

7 During the upstroke, notice how the wings bend in the middle. Some birds even bang their wings together at the top of the upstroke.

INSECT WINGS

Like all insects, a dragonfly's wings are thin and light. They are strengthened by a network of hollow tubes, called veins.

INSECTS' wings and birds' wings work in completely different ways. Insects' wings are flat and stiff. They do not have an airfoil shape. Instead, they churn the air to make swirling currents that provide lift. Forward movement comes from the wings pushing backward as they beat downward. Flying insects can hover and then dart off in any direction, twisting and turning through the air. They can even fly backward. Insects control their flight by beating their wings in extremely complicated patterns. Unlike most birds, an insect's upstroke is as powerful as the downstroke. Many flying insects, such as bees, wasps, and moths, have two pairs of wings; others, such as flies and mosquitoes, have only one.

Dragonflies

A dragonfly is one of the most skilled flying insects. Although most insects move their wings together, a dragonfly can move its two pairs separately.

As it beats its front wings down, it stirs up a whirlwind that passes over its back wings, generating lift. A segmented tail helps the dragonfly steer.

With each beat, a dragonfly's wings push air down and back to move the insect upward and forward, and they bend for more control during flight.

Butterflies
Butterflies have
two pairs of wings that
are hooked together so they act like one. The
wings are covered with powdery, colored scales.
Many butterflies have square-shaped wings that
flap slowly. The largest butterflies have wingspans
up to 10 inches (25 cm) across.

FACT BOX

• Insects beat their wings at different speeds.
The wings of a large dragonfly beat 35 times
a second; a housefly, 200 times a second; and
a mosquito, 600 times a second. The faster
the wings beat, the higher the buzzing sound.

• The dragonfly holds the record speed for
an insect at 55 miles (88.5 km) per hour.
A housefly can reach 3 ½ miles (5.6 km) per
hour, a mosquito ¾ mile (1.2 km) per hour.

• Monarch butterflies migrate more than
1,000 miles (1,600 km) each year.

• For its size, a dragonfly generates three times
the lift of the most efficient aircraft.

Beetles
A beetle's front wings are hard covers that protect the flying
wings underneath. In flight, the wing covers stick out, helping
to steady the beetle's body.

Flight muscles

Insect bodies
The body of a fly *(left)*
is like a hard box with all
the soft parts inside. A fly's
wings are attached to its
thorax, the central part
of the insect's body.
Hinged joints allow
each wing to move in
any direction. Large muscles
inside pull on the thorax,
moving the wings up
and down.

AMAZING FLYING ANIMALS

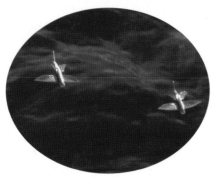

Close to the surface of the water, flying fish can swim very fast. They stretch out their wing-shaped fins, then leap upward and forward into the air, thrashing the water with their tails until they take off.

BESIDES birds and insects, the only other animals that can fly by flapping their wings are bats. Bats have wings that push downward to create lift. Unlike birds, most bats are nocturnal — they sleep during the day and fly at night. A few other kinds of animals can fly, but they do not power or control their flight with flapping wings. Flying frogs, flying lizards, and flying squirrels glide through the air in search of food or to escape from enemies. They jump out from high places and move forward through the air as they parachute downward. Flying fish sail through the air using two fins that look like wings. Their flights last only a few seconds, but they can glide much faster than they can swim.

FACT BOX

• Some flying fish can glide at 30 miles (48 km) per hour for several hundred yards (meters). The record flight for a flying fish is more than ½ mile (0.8 km) in 90 seconds.

• Flying foxes are actually large fruit-eating bats. More than 2,000 species of bats exist.

• Flying snakes flatten their bodies to help them glide from tree to tree.

• Some flying frogs jump from a height of 120 feet (36.6 m). They can glide about 90 feet (27 m) in only 8 seconds.

• The colugo, or flying lemur, can easily glide 300 feet (90 m) or more between trees.

Flying frogs
Flying frogs have enormous webbed feet, which they use as parachutes when they jump out of trees in search of insects. They can change the shape of their feet to control their flight. Sticky pads on their toes help them climb. With these pads, they can cling to the smoothest leaves and branches in the rain forest.

Flying lizards

A flying lizard has a flap of skin along each side of its body. This skin is stretched over spines hinged to the lizard's ribs. The spines stick out when danger threatens, and the lizard glides away.

Flying squirrels

Flying squirrels have folds of thin skin between their front and back legs. Stretching out their legs spreads the skin wide so they can glide from tree to tree.

Bat wings

A bat's wing is a sheet of flexible skin stretched between its fingers, the side of its body, and the back of its legs. Bats can adjust the shape of their wings much more than birds can. They twist and turn in the air like acrobats as they chase insects for food. The largest bats have wingspans up to 6 feet (1.8 m), but they weigh only about 2 pounds (1 kg).

PREHISTORIC FLYERS

THE dragonfly is the earliest known flying creature. The first dragonflies lived about 350 million years ago, during a hot, swampy era called the Carboniferous Period. Other flying insects evolved during the following 150 million years, many of them similar to the insects we know today. The first gliding reptiles appeared about 200 million years ago. From these gliders came pterosaurs, which were giant flying lizards, some with wingspans up to 36 feet (11 m). The first feathered creature, called *Archaeopteryx*, lived over 150 million years ago. Some scientists think it evolved from small dinosaurs, and it might be the first known bird.

This insect (above) *lived about 50 million years ago. It got caught in sticky tree resin that gradually fossilized into amber.*

FACT BOX

• Some prehistoric dragonflies had wingspans up to 3 feet (1 m).

• Some of the first humans lived about 1.5 million years ago. Modern-looking birds have existed for over 30 million years.

• Modern birds have only two finger bones in each wing. *Archaeopteryx* had all five bones, complete with claws at the ends.

• Fish fossils are often found near pterosaurs, so these flying lizards might have lived at sea.

• A pterosaur called *Quetzalcoatlus* is the largest flying animal that has ever existed. It had a human-sized body and a wingspan of 36 feet (11 m) — wider than a hang glider!

Gliding reptiles

The first flying reptiles were gliders. *Longisquama (above)* had tall crests along its back that might have opened up like wings to help it glide.

Giant pterosaurs

Pterosaurs were the first true flying reptiles. They lived at the same time as dinosaurs, and some of them were huge. Their wings were covered with skin, but their bodies were usually furry. Their light, delicate bones reduced their weight, which helped them fly.

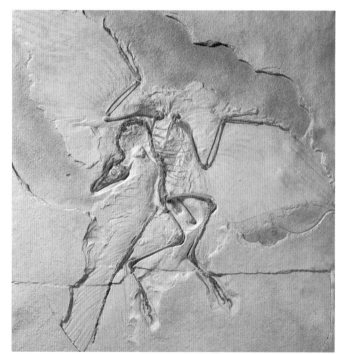

Archaeopteryx

Archaeopteryx had wings and legs like a bird, but its mouth was full of teeth, and its tail looked like a lizard's. It had thick feathers, but many scientists do not think it could fly very well. The first *Archaeopteryx* fossil was found in a quarry in Germany in 1860. Since then, six more have been discovered.

Fossilized feathers

This fossil *(above)* is the skeleton of an *Archaeopteryx*. When the animal died, its skin and flesh rotted away, and its skeleton, buried deep underground, slowly turned to stone.

AIRCRAFT WINGS

This aircraft (above) is called a triplane because it has three sets of wings. Early planes were slow, so they needed more sets of wings to provide enough lift.

THE smallest ultralight carries one person and weighs less than 200 pounds (90 kg). The largest passenger jet carries over 500 people and weighs about 437 tons (397 metric tons). Whatever the size or shape, all airplanes have one thing in common — wings. Wings provide the lift aircraft need to fly. The shape of an aircraft's wings depends on how fast and how high it must fly. Swept-back wings are needed for high-speed flight. Broad wings are needed to carry heavy loads. All wings have moving parts to help the aircraft take off, land, and change direction.

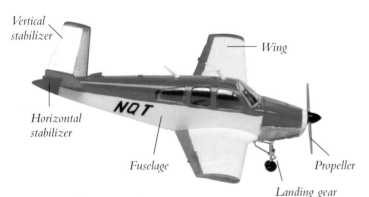

Vertical stabilizer

Wing

Horizontal stabilizer

NQT

Fuselage

Propeller

Landing gear

The parts of an aircraft
This picture *(above)* identifies the main parts of a small aircraft. These parts are needed for the aircraft to take off, fly level, change direction, and land. The body of the aircraft is called the fuselage, and the wheels are called the landing gear. On many aircraft, the landing gear folds up inside the fuselage during flight to reduce drag. Hinged control surfaces on the tail and the wings help steer the aircraft from left to right or up and down.

Piper Cadet
This small aircraft *(above)* is called a monoplane because it has one set of wings. It flies rather slowly; so, to provide enough lift, its wings stick straight out from the aircraft's body.

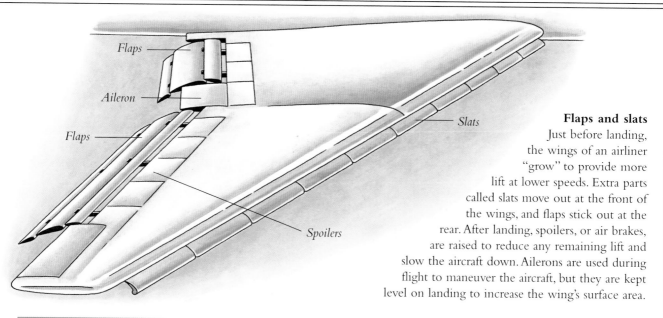

Flaps

Aileron

Flaps

Slats

Spoilers

Flaps and slats
Just before landing, the wings of an airliner "grow" to provide more lift at lower speeds. Extra parts called slats move out at the front of the wings, and flaps stick out at the rear. After landing, spoilers, or air brakes, are raised to reduce any remaining lift and slow the aircraft down. Ailerons are used during flight to maneuver the aircraft, but they are kept level on landing to increase the wing's surface area.

Boeing 747
The Boeing 747 flies high and fast. Its large wings provide enough lift to carry more than 400 tons (363 metric tons). The wings are tapered and swept back to keep drag low when flying 600 miles (965 km) per hour. Because swept-back wings reduce lift, this jet needs a high takeoff speed.

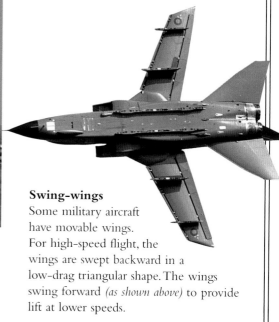

Swing-wings
Some military aircraft have movable wings. For high-speed flight, the wings are swept backward in a low-drag triangular shape. The wings swing forward (*as shown above*) to provide lift at lower speeds.

FLYING AN AIRPLANE

Biplanes have two sets of wings. They are strong, agile, and easy to fly, so they are often used as trainer planes or in acrobatic displays. Until the 1930s, most biplanes had open cockpits, and their wings were braced with wires and struts.

To steer a car, all you have to do is turn the steering wheel. To steer a plane, you have to move two sets of controls — one with your hands, and one with your feet — to adjust the control surfaces on the plane's wings and tail. Control surfaces are small, hinged flaps that determine how air will flow around the plane. The three main types of control surfaces are: the ailerons attached to the back edge of each wing, the elevators mounted at the rear of the tailplane, and the rudder at the rear of the tail fin. Flight can also be controlled with engine power — more power increases speed, which increases lift. So, an accelerating aircraft, flying level, will steadily gain height.

Aileron

Aileron

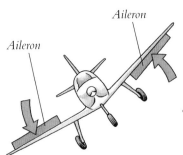

Elevator

Rudder

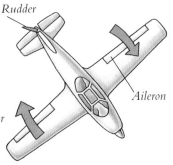

Aileron

Control surfaces
To turn an aircraft (yaw), the pilot moves the rudder to one side. To make an aircraft climb or descend (pitch), the pilot adjusts the elevators on the tailplane. To roll an aircraft to the right or left (tilt or bank), the pilot raises the aileron on one wing and lowers it on the other.

Roll

The ailerons on an aircraft work the opposite of each other. When one aileron is raised, the other is lowered. The wing with the lowered aileron rises; the wing with the raised aileron drops.

Pitch

The elevators on a plane's tail are raised or lowered to make the plane's nose rise or fall. Lowering the elevators puts the nose down, causing the plane to dive. Raising the elevators puts the nose up, and the plane climbs.

Yaw

A plane's rudder can be swiveled to one side or the other to move the aircraft left or right. The plane's nose points in the same direction the rudder points. The rudder and ailerons are used together to turn the plane.

Turning

When an aircraft turns, it moves somewhat like a cyclist going around a corner. It banks as it turns, which means it leans to one side with one wing higher than the other, using some of the lift from the wings to help it turn smoothly.

Inside the cockpit of a modern small aircraft, the pilot uses throttle levers to adjust engine power. The control column and pedals move the control surfaces. Dials and gauges show information about fuel consumption, flight direction, altitude, and how level the plane is flying.

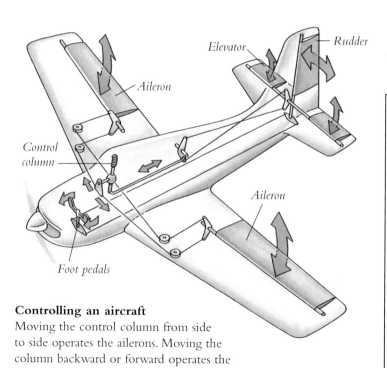

Elevator

Rudder

Aileron

Control column

Aileron

Foot pedals

Controlling an aircraft

Moving the control column from side to side operates the ailerons. Moving the column backward or forward operates the elevators. Foot pedals move the rudder from side to side.

FACT BOX

• Many flight terms are borrowed from terms used on ships, for example, rudder, port (left side), and starboard (right side).

• An airliner takes one minute and about 1 mile (1.6 km) of airspace to reverse course.

• A cruising airliner loses 3 tons (2.7 metric tons) of weight per hour as it uses up fuel.

• Many aircraft use computer-controlled autopilot systems that automatically set the controls for takeoff and landing.

• When flying a helicopter, the pilot adjusts the angle of the rotor blades to hover or to go straight upward, forward, backward, or sideways.

MAKE A MODEL PLANE

THE two previous pages explain how the control surfaces on the wings and tail of an aircraft work. They change the way air flows over the aircraft, allowing the pilot to steer it in different directions. Working together, the ailerons and rudder turn the plane left or right. The elevators on the tail raise and lower the nose of the plane. These two pages show you how to make a model plane, so you can see for yourself how the control surfaces work. Although a model is much smaller than a full-size aircraft, it flies in exactly the same way. The scientific rules of flying are the same for any aircraft, whether it is an airliner weighing 437 tons (397 metric tons) or a simple model made of paper, tape, and a drinking straw.

You will need:
pencil, paper, ruler, scissors, glue stick,
tape, drinking straw, paper clip.

Make a model plane

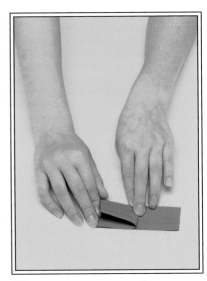

1 Draw two paper rectangles, 10 x 4 inches (25 x 10 cm) and 9 x 2 inches (22.5 x 5 cm). On the large one, draw two ailerons; on the small one, elevators and a center line.

2 Cut out the rectangles. Fold the large one over a pencil. Glue down the top edge along the line drawn for the ailerons. Make cuts so the ailerons can move.

3 Fold the small rectangle into a *W* shape. Glue the center together to make an upright tail fin. Make cuts so the rudder and elevators can move.

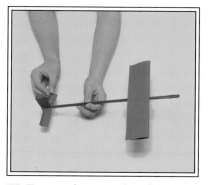

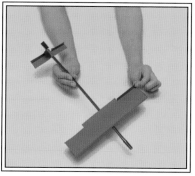

4 Tape the wings and tail to a straw, which is the plane's fuselage. Position the wings about three-quarters of the way up the fuselage from the tail.

5 Try out the control surfaces. Bending the elevators up slightly will make the plane climb as it flies. Bending the elevators down will make it dive.

6 Bending the left aileron up and the right aileron down, by the same amount, and bending the rudder to the left, will make the plane turn to the left as it flies.

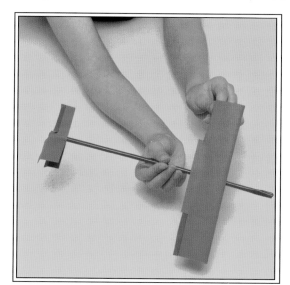

7 Bending the right aileron up, the left aileron down, and the rudder to the right will make the plane turn to the right. Can you make the plane fly in a circle?

8 To fly the plane, throw it straight ahead. To make it fly well, weigh the nose down using a paper clip or modeling clay.

PROPELLERS

ALL aircraft need thrust to push them through the air. Propellers whirling at high speeds turn the power of an aircraft's engine into thrust. Propellers have two or more blades, each shaped like a long, thin airfoil wing. These blades generate lift in a forward direction as they slice through the air. Modern propellers have variable-pitch blades that allow the pilot to adjust the angle at which the blades cut into the air. Changing the pitch of a propeller is like changing gears on a bicycle. For takeoff, the blades face forward and the engine spins very fast to generate maximum thrust. Cruising requires less thrust, so the blades are set at a sharper angle, and the engine spins more slowly. This arrangement also uses fuel more economically.

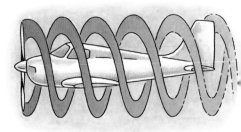

Propellers spiral their way through the air similar to the way a screw goes into wood. For this reason, aircraft with propellers are sometimes called "airscrews." As a propeller turns, its blades push the air backward, producing thrust and moving the aircraft forward.

DH-88 Comet
In 1934, the DeHavilland DH-88 Comet took part in a race from England to Australia. The Comet *(above)* was restored for the fiftieth anniversary of the race. Each propeller is driven by its own engine, which is like a huge car engine, and is fueled by gasoline.

Wooden propellers
Propellers on the first airplanes were layers of wood glued together. The pilot had to spin the propeller by hand to start the engine — a dangerous job, because the pilot could be hit.

Ultralights

If you attach an engine-driven propeller to a hang glider, the result is an ultralight *(right)*. An ultralight's engine produces about the same amount of power as a small family car. The propeller has twin blades and is less than 3 feet (1 m) across. It pushes the plane along at about 36 miles (58 km) per hour.

Lockheed Hercules

This aircraft *(below)* carries military supplies. Each propeller has four variable-pitch blades. The propellers are driven by a turboprop engine, which is a type of jet engine.

Piper Seneca

Each propeller on this four-seater plane *(above)* has two blades that are twisted at an angle, like the blades of a fan. As the propellers spin, the blades force air backward.

MAKE A PROPELLER

You will need:
thin paper, pencil, ruler,
scissors, paper clip.

A propeller works in two different ways at the same time. As it spins, it makes air move past it. In propeller-driven aircraft, this movement produces thrust. At the same time, air moving past a propeller makes the propeller spin. The projects on these two pages show how propellers work in these two ways. In the first project, you can make a simple paper propeller, called a spinner. As the spinner falls, moving air rushes past its blades, making the spinner twirl. In the second project, you can make a spinning propeller fly upward through the air. The propeller blades are positioned at an angle, similar to the blades of a fan. As the blades whirl around, they move the air, producing thrust that lifts the propeller upward. Children in China first flew propellers like this 600 years ago.

Make a spinner

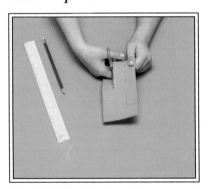

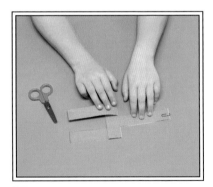

1 Draw a *T* shape *(as shown)* on a piece of thin paper that is 6 inches (15 cm) long and 4 inches (10 cm) wide. Cut along the two long lines of the *T*.

2 Fold along the two short lines *(as shown)* to make two blades. Attach a paper clip at the bottom of the stem. Now, open the blades flat and drop the spinner.

To make the spinner twirl faster, twist each blade before dropping it again.

Make a propeller

1 With a compass, draw a 4-inch (10-cm) circle on cardboard. Draw a 1-inch (2.5-cm) circle in the center of the larger circle. With a protractor, draw lines dividing the circle into 16 equal sections.

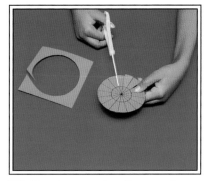

2 Cut along section lines, to the small circle, to form blades. Twist each blade slightly to angle it.

M A T E R I A L S

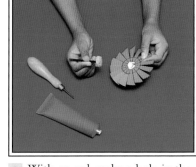

You will need: compass, ruler, thick cardboard, protractor, pen, scissors, awl, ½-inch (1.2-cm) slice of cork, dowel, glue, string, thread spool.

3 With an awl, make a hole in the center of a slice of cork. Put glue on one end of a dowel and push it into the hole. Glue the cork to the center of the propeller.

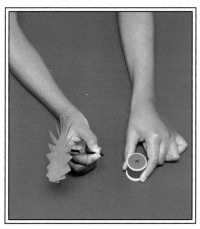

4 When the glue is dry, wind a long piece of string around the dowel. Put the dowel into the thread spool — and try a test flight!

5 Pull the string to spin the propeller. When the string comes off, the blades should have produced enough thrust to lift the propeller into the air.

43

JET ENGINES

Most large modern aircraft are powered by jet engines. Jet-propelled aircraft fly faster than propeller-driven aircraft, and they can fly higher, where the air is thin and drag is reduced. Jet engines have huge fans inside that draw in air and compress it. Burning fuel produces a roaring jet of hot gases that blasts out from the rear of the engine, producing thrust. Some military aircraft rely on turbojet engines, which are very powerful, but noisy, and they use enormous amounts of fuel. Passenger jets use turbofan engines. These engines have an extra-large fan in the front. This fan produces most of the engine's thrust by forcing air around the engine so it can combine with the jet of exhaust gases at the rear.

An octopus uses jet propulsion to move fast. It draws in water, then squeezes it out through a small hole. The jet of water this creates pushes the octopus along.

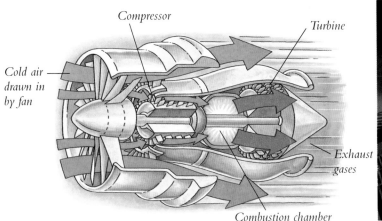

Compressor

Turbine

Cold air drawn in by fan

Exhaust gases

Combustion chamber

A turbofan engine
A jet engine is tube shaped and has a fast-spinning fan that pulls air into the engine. Fuel burns in the air and heats it. Exhaust gases spin the turbine that drives the compressor. Expanding gases leave the engine at over 6,000 feet (1,800 m) per second. This blast of hot gases pushes the engine, and the aircraft, forward.

Inside a jet engine
This jet engine *(above)* has had its protective cowling removed for an inspection. The huge blades you can see at the front draw in air as they turn. Most of the small pipes supply fuel and lubricating oil to the parts inside the engine.

Executive jets

Commuter jets *(above)* carry people on business trips. Their engines are on their tails, not on their wings. Many of them can fly as fast as a large airliner.

The Blackbird

The Lockheed SR-71 Blackbird reconnaissance plane is powered by turbojet engines. In 1974, one flew from New York to London in 1 hour, 54 minutes — an unbroken record of 2,000 miles (3,218 km) per hour. In the 1970s and 1980s, the U.S. Air Force used these jets to fly at high altitudes and take aerial photographs of enemy territory.

Jumbo jets

The Boeing 747, introduced in 1970, was the very first wide-bodied jet. It has made international jet travel very common.

Helicopters

Helicopters have turboshaft engines, a type of jet engine without a jet of gases. Most of this engine's power turns the helicopter's rotors; only a little of it pushes the aircraft forward.

JETS AND TURBINES

A jet engine looks complicated, but the way it works is very simple. A jet moving in one direction produces thrust in the other direction. Imagine you are standing on a skateboard and squirting a powerful hose forward. Jet propulsion will push you backward. Knowledge of this reaction has existed for nearly 2,000 years, but it was not until the 1930s that it was used in an engine. In the projects on these two pages, you can make a jet that zooms along a string and find out how a turbine works. The jet in the first project is a balloon that produces thrust from escaping air. The second project shows you how to make a turbine and use hot air to turn its blades. When you try this project, be sure to have an adult light the candles. Although these projects might seem very simple, they use the same scientific principles that propel all jet airplanes.

Make a balloon jet

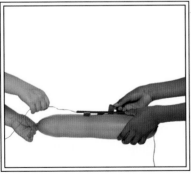

1 Inflate the balloon and keep a tight hold on the neck while you tape the straw to the top of it. Thread the string through the straw and stretch the string across the room.

2 Let go of the neck of the balloon. A stream of air rushes out, producing thrust that propels the balloon forward along the string. Inflate the balloon again and try another flight.

Make a turbine

1 Cut out the bottom of a large aluminum pie plate and use a compass to draw a small circle in the center of it.

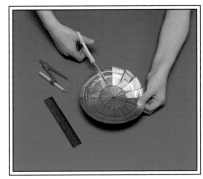

2 Use a protractor to divide the circle into 16 equal sections. Cut along each section line, to the edge of the small circle, to form blades.

3 Twist the blades slightly to angle them. You now have completed the turbine. The rest of the project shows you how to make it turn.

MATERIALS

You will need: scissors, aluminum pie plate, compass, protractor, tape, pin, dowel, bead, thread spool, modeling clay, plate, 4 candles, matches.

6 Make a hole in the center of the turbine and place it on the pin. Ask an adult to light the candles. Hot air will spin the turbine's blades.

4 Tape the blunt end of a pin to one end of a dowel. Put a bead on the pin.

5 Put the dowel into a spool, anchor the spool in clay on a plate, and put candles around it.

BREAKING THE SOUND BARRIER

THE sound barrier is like an invisible wall that travels in front of a speeding aircraft. Where does it come from? As an airplane flies, it creates pressure waves in the air that are like ripples in the water around a moving boat. These waves move away from the aircraft at the speed of sound. When the aircraft is traveling at the speed of sound, the waves cannot outrun it, so they build up and compress the air in front of the aircraft creating a shock wave. An aircraft that flies faster than the speed of sound flies through this barrier of compressed air. When an aircraft goes through the sound barrier, there sometimes is a jolt, because drag suddenly increases. The shock wave spreads out and can be heard on the ground as a loud rumble, called a sonic boom.

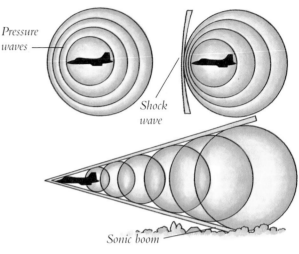

Pressure waves

Shock wave

Sonic boom

A flying aircraft sends out pressure waves that move at the speed of sound. When the aircraft flies at the speed of sound, a shock wave builds up in front of it. An aircraft accelerating through the sound barrier causes a sonic boom.

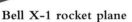

Bell X-1 rocket plane
In 1947, the rocket-powered Bell X-1 was the first aircraft to travel faster than the speed of sound, or Mach 1.

The Bell X-1 was dropped from a B29 bomber at 23,000 feet (7,000 m). At 42,000 feet (12,800 m), it broke through the sound barrier.

Pilot's-eye view
A large transparent canopy gives a fighter pilot a good view. Fighter pilots need many computers in the cockpit to handle the enormous amount of information required to fly jet fighter planes.

Jet fighter
The Mirage *(below)* flies at more than twice the speed of sound. It climbs almost straight upward and can reach the same height as a cruising airliner in about one minute. This supersonic jet is used by air forces around the world. Different models can be used as fighters, fighter bombers, and for reconnaissance.

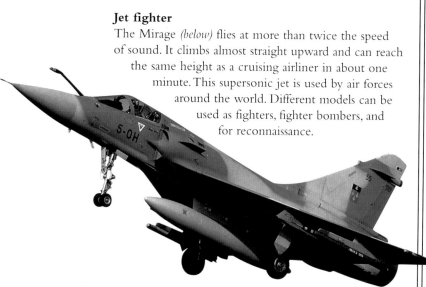

Concorde
The Concorde is the world's only supersonic passenger airliner. It cruises at 1,300 miles (2,100 km) per hour, more than twice the speed of an ordinary airliner. It can cross the Atlantic Ocean in about three hours. It is noisy, however, and uses a lot of fuel.

FACT BOX

• The speed of sound changes with air temperature and density. Mach 1 is 735 miles (1,183 km) per hour at sea level (68°F/20°C) but only 636 miles (1,023 km) per hour at 36,000 feet (11,000 m), where the air is colder (12°F/-11°C).

• Subsonic speeds are below Mach 0.8 (jumbo jets). Transonic speeds (Mach 0.8 to Mach 1.2) break the sound barrier. Supersonic speeds are Mach 1.2 to Mach 5 (the Concorde and fighter jets). Hypersonic speeds are above Mach 5 (space shuttle).

• The Russian Tupolev Tu-144, a supersonic civilian aircraft, first flew on December 31, 1968 — two months before the Concorde.

GOING UP

Watch a bird take off. It just flaps its wings, and up it goes! A modern airliner must charge down a runway like a race car and has to travel nearly 2 miles (3.2 km) before it reaches takeoff speed, when its wings lift it off the ground. Special types of aircraft, however, are designed to take off and land on a single spot. They are called Vertical Takeoff and Landing aircraft, or VTOL. Examples include the Harrier jump jet and an early prototype, nicknamed the *Flying Bedstead* because of its peculiar appearance. Helicopters, too, are VTOL aircraft, but they are slow compared to airplanes and use a lot of fuel. Other aircraft are designed to use very short runways, only a few hundred yards (m) long. They are called Short Takeoff and Landing aircraft, or STOL. STOL aircraft can fly from airports in the middle of cities or from remote airstrips in fields or deserts.

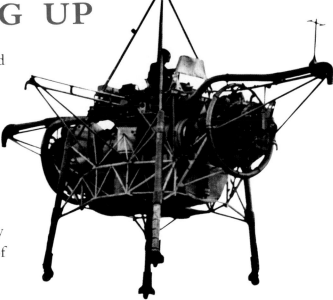

The Flying Bedstead, *from the 1950s, was built to experiment with ideas about vertical flight. Moving nozzles directed the thrust from a jet engine. Experiments with this machine helped design the Harrier jump jet.*

Forward flight

Transition to forward flight

Takeoff

Harrier jump jet
The engine of a jump jet has four nozzles attached to its exhaust system. At takeoff, the nozzles direct thrust downward, so the plane goes straight up. The nozzles swivel backward to move the jet forward.

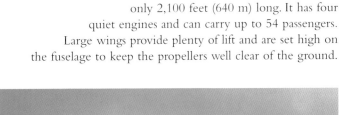

DeHavilland Dash 7
The Dash is used on short runways in cities. It can take off on a runway only 2,100 feet (640 m) long. It has four quiet engines and can carry up to 54 passengers. Large wings provide plenty of lift and are set high on the fuselage to keep the propellers well clear of the ground.

Autogyros
An autogyro is a cross between an airplane and a helicopter. Its rotor is not driven by an engine. During flight, rushing air spins the rotor, which provides most of the lift to keep the autogyro up in the air.

Bell-Boeing Osprey
The Osprey is a tilt-rotor aircraft. Its giant propellers, called proprotors, are mounted at the tips of its wings and tilt upward to take off like a helicopter. For forward flight, the proprotors swing down into an airplane propeller position. The Osprey can fly three times as far as a helicopter on the same amount of fuel.

STRANGE AIRCRAFT

ANY aircraft look strange. The Belluga transport plane looks like a huge dolphin with wings. The fabric on the wings of a pedal-powered aircraft is so thin that light shines through it. An aircraft's strange appearance means it has been specially designed for a particular purpose. The Belluga is designed to carry large items that will not fit into the cargo hold of an ordinary transport airplane. Pedal-powered aircraft must be ultralight, so their wings are made with a thin plastic covering. People called aeronautical engineers design new planes for many different purposes — to carry enormous loads, to fly very fast, or even to fly nonstop around the world. For any purpose, an aircraft, no matter how strange it looks, must be designed to take off, fly, and land safely.

The Optica observation plane was designed for low-speed flight and to provide a wide, clear view for observing such things as traffic flow problems or crop growth.

Pedal power
The first successful pedal-powered aircraft, *Gossamer Albatross (above)*, had wings of thin plastic stretched on ribs only ½ inch (1.2 cm) thick to make the plane very light.

World voyager
In 1986, Americans Jeana Yeager and Dick Rutan flew *Voyager (above)* nonstop around the world in nine days — without refueling. Each wing of this specially built plane was four times the length of the fuselage, providing the greatest lift with the lowest drag.

Invisible fighter

The F-117 Stealth Fighter *(left)* has flat, slab-shaped panels made of special materials. These panels scatter beams from enemy radar, making the plane almost undetectable. Ordinary planes can be detected because they reflect radar beams straight back. The F-117's low, flat shape reflects the beams in other directions. It also has special paint to absorb some of the beams.

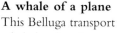

A whale of a plane

This Belluga transport plane *(left)* is the size of a whale but has the streamlined shape of a dolphin to reduce drag. Its cargo hold is 24 feet (7 m) high and can carry almost 25 tons (23 metric tons).

Solar power

Solar Challenger (left), the world's first successful solar-powered aircraft, is, at 125 pounds (56.7 kg), the lightest powered aircraft. Solar cells on the wings make electricity from sunlight. An electric motor drives the propellers.

FACT BOX

• In 1907, one of the first powered flights in Britain was made in a bizarre-looking multiplane called the *Venetian Blind*. It had nearly fifty sets of wings.

• The aircraft with the longest wingspan was a flying boat called the *Spruce Goose*, designed by eccentric millionaire Howard Hughes. It had a wingspan of over 300 feet (90 m) and made its first and only flight in November 1947.

• Some large, propeller-driven planes can scoop up huge amounts of water from lakes, then drop the water like a bomb to put out forest fires.

FLYING THROUGH WATER

This boat has hydrofoils to lift its hull out of the water. At low speeds or stopped, it floats on the water like a normal boat.

WINGS can work under water as well as in the air. Some boats have underwater wings, called hydrofoils. As the boat speeds along, the hydrofoils lift it up out of the water. The hull of the boat is then traveling through the air, and drag is greatly reduced. Hydrofoil boats can go over 60 miles (96 km) per hour, more than three times as fast as an ordinary boat. Propeller-driven hovercraft also virtually fly across the sea — over 72 miles (116 km) per hour. Powerful fans blow air down through a rubber skirt to provide a cushion of air that keeps the hovercraft about an inch (2.5 cm) above the water's surface, reducing friction between the boat and the water below.

You will need: the lid of a plastic margarine container, scissors, stapler, awl, pliers, coat hanger wire (ask an adult to cut out the bottom section).

How a hydrofoil works

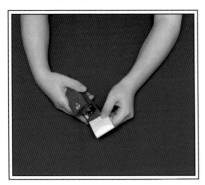

1 Cut a rectangle, 2 x 4 inches (5 x 10 cm), from the plastic lid. Fold it in half to make a hydrofoil and staple the ends together ½ inch (1.2 cm) in from the back edge.

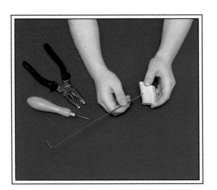

2 Use an awl to make two holes in the front of the hydrofoil, ½ inch (1.2 cm) in from the front edge. Use pliers to bend one end of the wire. Slide the hydrofoil onto the wire.

3 Move the hydrofoil through the air — it does not lift up. Pull it through water — it climbs up the wire.

How a hovercraft works

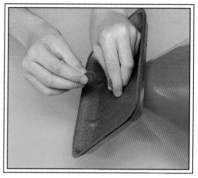

1 Use a pencil to poke a hole through the middle of a polystyrene tray. The hole should be about ½ inch (1.2 cm) across.

2 Inflate the balloon and pinch its neck to keep the air from escaping. Pull the neck of the balloon through the hole in the tray.

3 Keep pinching the balloon's neck while you put the button into it. The button will control how fast the air escapes.

MATERIALS

You will need:
a polystyrene tray,
pencil, balloon,
balloon pump, button.

4 Set the tray down on a table. As air escapes from the balloon under the tray, it lifts the tray slightly off the table. If you give the tray a gentle push, it will skate along.

This hovercraft's rubber skirt is the black part just above the water. The air cushion makes the water spray out around the skirt. Four large propellers drive the hovercraft in any direction.

ROCKETS AND SPACEFLIGHT

WHY can't an airplane fly off into space? The main reason is that there is no air in space. Wings need air to provide lift. Because air becomes thinner higher up, airplanes cannot fly above approximately 120,000 feet (36,600 m). Jets need oxygen from the air to burn fuel, but there is not enough oxygen for them to work properly above approximately 65,000 feet (20,000 m). Rockets can fly in space because they carry oxygen with them. There are two main types of rockets: liquid-fuel and solid-fuel. Liquid-fuel rockets carry liquid oxygen to burn their fuel (liquid hydrogen). Solid-fuel rockets are like enormous fireworks. They contain chemicals that release oxygen when heated.

Blast-off
The space shuttle has three liquid-fuel engines that burn a mixture of liquid oxygen and liquid hydrogen from a strapped-on tank. Extra thrust comes from two solid-fuel booster rockets. The tank and boosters fall away when the fuel is used up.

Landing shuttle
The space shuttle takes off like a rocket, but lands like a glider. It glides down toward a runway just like an ordinary aircraft and deploys a parachute to help it roll to a stop. Each shuttle is expected to make one hundred launches in its lifetime.

FACT BOX

- Liquid oxygen is stored at -297.4°F (-183°C); liquid hydrogen at -427°F (-255°C). Temperatures at the South Pole are only about -40°F (-40°C).

- The space shuttle's engines create 2,200 tons (2,000 metric tons) of thrust at takeoff — 20 times more than a jet airliner's engines.

- To escape Earth's gravity, a rocket must reach "escape velocity," a speed of about 7 miles (11 km) per second.

- Solid-fuel rockets were invented in China nearly 1,000 years ago. They were fueled by gunpowder and were used to scare enemies.

Syncom

Syncom *(right)*, a communication satellite that relays radio and TV signals all around the world, was taken into space by the shuttle and is held in orbit by Earth's gravity. It travels at a speed that is fast enough to keep it from falling back to Earth.

Ariane

A three-stage rocket, Ariane has three rockets mounted one above the other. After takeoff, the first stage falls away when its fuel is used up. The second stage then fires, followed by the third.

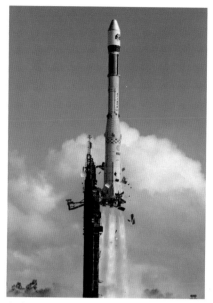

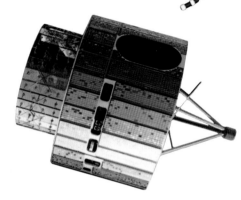

Meteosat

Meteosat *(left)*, a weather satellite, was carried into space by the shuttle. From the shuttle's low Earth orbit, a small rocket pushed Meteosat 21,000 miles (33,790 km) farther out. From this distance, it can send back pictures of half of Earth's surface.

Inside a rocket

Liquid hydrogen and liquid oxygen are pumped into a combustion chamber where the hydrogen burns furiously in the oxygen, creating exhaust that produces tremendous thrust.

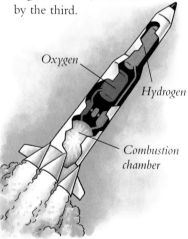

Oxygen

Hydrogen

Combustion chamber

Probing into space

This picture *(above)* shows the space probe *Galileo* nearing the planet Jupiter in 1995. Launched by the shuttle, *Galileo* used the gravity of the planets to move toward its destination.

MAKE A ROCKET

Rockets have powerful engines. They can carry satellites into orbit more than 200 miles (320 km) above Earth's surface.

S PACE rockets rely on jet propulsion to fly. As a stream of hot gases roars out its tail end, the rocket surges forward. The thrust of a rocket depends on the amount of propellant it shoots out every second. Deep in the sea, octopuses also rely on jet propulsion. To escape from their enemies, they squirt out a jet of water and shoot off in the opposite direction. Water is a better propellant than hot gas because it is so much heavier. This project shows you how to make and fly a rocket that uses jet propulsion. If you follow the instructions carefully, your rocket could fly more than 75 feet (23 m) above the ground. This rocket is very powerful. Ask an adult to help you make some parts of the rocket and be sure an adult is with you when you launch it. When you do a test flight, set up the rocket in an open space, well away from trees and buildings. Do not stand over the rocket while it is being launched — and wear clothes you do not mind getting very wet!

MATERIALS

You will need:
plain and colored cardboard, pen, scissors, plastic bottle, tape, funnel, container of water, awl, cork, air valve, plastic tubing, bicycle pump.

Make a rocket

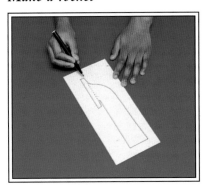

1 Rockets need fins to fly straight. Draw a fin pattern about 8 inches (20 cm) long on plain cardboard. Cut it out and use it to make four fins from colored cardboard.

2 Decorate a plastic bottle to look like a rocket. Fold over the tab at the top of each fin and use long pieces of tape to attach the fins firmly to the bottle.

3 Use a funnel to half fill the bottle with water. (The water is the propellant. Compressed air above the water will provide the energy that creates thrust.)

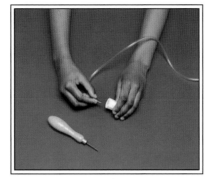

4 Use an awl to drill a hole through a cork. Push the wide end of an air valve into a piece of plastic tubing. Push the valve through the hole in the cork.

5 Push the cork into the neck of the bottle. Make sure it is pushed in firmly so the cork does not come out too easily.

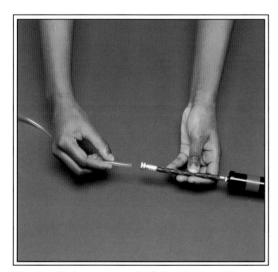

6 Attach the open end of the plastic tubing to a bicycle pump. Stand the rocket on its tail fins — you are ready to launch! Look for a launch site outside, well away from trees and buildings — and ask an adult to help.

7 Start pumping air into the rocket with a bicycle pump. Bubbles of air will rise through the water. When the pressure inside the bottle is great enough, the cork and the water will be forced out and the rocket will shoot upward.

THE HISTORY OF FLIGHT

SINCE ancient times, human beings have wished they could fly. The first people to get off the ground were the Chinese. Over 700 years ago, they used kites to lift people into the air. In the eighteenth century, lighter-than-air balloons carried their first passengers, and, in 1852, the world's first airship flight took place. It was not, however, until the invention of the gasoline engine in the 1880s that true powered flight in a heavier-than-air machine became possible. In 1903, the Wright brothers made the world's first powered, controlled, and sustained flight in their aircraft, *Flyer 1*.

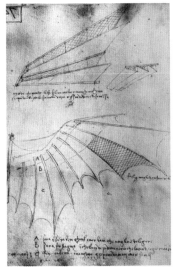

About 500 years ago, Italian artist and inventor Leonardo da Vinci drew many designs for flying machines. His scientific ideas about flight were correct, but a human could not provide enough power to make them work.

Clément Ader

In 1890, Ader's *Eole (right),* a steam-driven aircraft, became the first full-size airplane to leave the ground, but the 150 feet (45 m) it managed to hop was not powered flight because it was not controlled.

Otto Lilienthal

In the 1890s, German experimenter Otto Lilienthal built hang gliders from reeds covered with shirt fabric. He was the first person to make repeated controlled flights, more than 2,000 of them, and he showed how curved airfoil wings work better than flat ones. Unfortunately, while making a test flight, Lilienthal crash-landed and died.

Orville and Wilbur Wright

On December 17, 1903, American inventor Orville Wright flew *Flyer 1* a distance of 108 feet (33 m) at an altitude of about 9 feet (3 m). He was the first person to make a controlled, powered takeoff, flight, and landing.

Louis Blériot

In 1909, Frenchman Louis Blériot became the first person to fly across the English Channel. The trip took 37 minutes, flying at an average speed of 36 miles (58 km) per hour. This picture *(above)* shows a modern replica of his plane.

Charles Lindbergh

In 1927, American Charles Lindbergh was the first person to fly alone, and nonstop, across the Atlantic Ocean. The flight from New York to Paris in his tiny Ryan monoplane, *The Spirit of St. Louis*, took 33 hours and 39 minutes. He flew 3,600 miles (5,800 km) at an average speed of 120 miles (193 km) per hour.

FACT BOX

- **1908:** Orville Wright made the first sustained, powered flight. It lasted one hour.
- **1937:** British engineer Frank Whittle designed the jet engine.
- **1947:** the first aircraft flew at supersonic speed in the United States.
- **1952:** the first jet airliner, the DeHavilland Comet, began flight service in England.
- **1970:** the Boeing 747 jumbo jet began flight service.
- **1976:** the Concorde began transatlantic flight service.

FLIGHT INTO THE FUTURE

BIRDS have been flying for more than 30 million years. Humans first took to the air only 200 years ago. Today, the sky is full of aircraft of all descriptions. Some planes fly three times faster than the speed of sound. A flight halfway around the world can take less than twenty-four hours. What does the future hold? What will be in the sky ten years from now? Engineers are developing more powerful engines, resin materials lighter and stronger than metal, and unusual new wing shapes to help aircraft fly faster and higher. Whatever happens, human flight will increase — but at what cost to the health of our environment and the birds and animals that share it?

The Boeing 747-400 can carry up to 567 passengers. It is a double-decker version of the 1970s jumbo jet. Plans for a super-jumbo jet, the 747-600X, have been canceled due to cost.

Horizontal Takeoff and Landing (HOTOL)
This picture is an artist's impression of HOTOL riding piggyback to 45,000 feet (13,700 m) on Antonin 225, the world's largest airplane. HOTOL then uses rocket engines to fly into space. At Mach 5, it could fly from England to Australia in less than four hours.

FACT BOX

• A Russian experimental plane, called an ekranoplan, has been designed to gain extra lift by skimming across the surface of the ocean. Reports indicate that an ekranoplan uses far less fuel than a conventional aircraft.

• All new airplanes must meet strict environmental rules governing noise levels and emissions that might further damage the sensitive ozone layer.

• Modern cockpits use advanced electronic systems to reduce the pilot's workload. While optical fibers carry signals at the speed of light to the aircraft's control surfaces, holographic displays and keyboards project data onto a see-through screen.

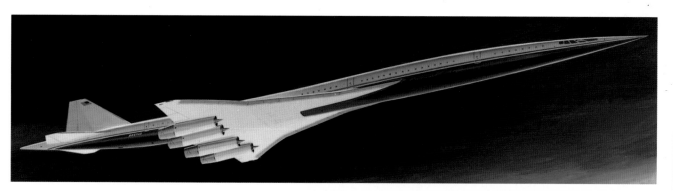

High Speed Civil Transport (HSCT)

This airliner *(above)*, flying at Mach 3, might one day carry 200 passengers from New York to Tokyo in about three hours. It will cruise above 54,000 feet (16,500 m) and will have engines that will not damage the ozone layer.

X-30
space plane

Aircraft can travel extremely fast in space because there is no air to create drag. This model *(right)* shows what the X-30 might look like. It would fly through the edge of space at speeds up to Mach 5 to reach its destination.

X-29 experimental plane

The experimental X-29 aircraft *(above)* refuels in midair from a tanker plane. The X-29 has unusual swept-forward wings that provide high lift and low drag, making it very maneuverable. Tests with the X-29 could lead to new designs for passenger planes.

GLOSSARY

aileron – a movable surface on the back edge of an airplane wing that helps control and maneuver the plane, especially when rolling, or banking, the plane to the right or left.

airfoil – a wing-shaped form with a curved upper surface that, when moving through the air, creates an upward push, or lift, underneath to hold it up.

airship – an aircraft that is lighter than air, like a hot-air balloon, but is powered by an engine and propellers and has a steering system.

albatross – one of the largest web-footed seabirds with an enormous wingspan that creates enough lift to keep it gliding on rising air currents for hours.

altitude – a measure of vertical distance, or height, above the ground.

boomerang – a piece of wood with an airfoil shape and bent in the middle, so that, when it is thrown forward, it will come back to the thrower.

bridle – a line or cord with each end attached at opposite sides of an object to distribute the force of something pulling on the object.

canopy – the part of a parachute that fills up with air (the fabric); also, the transparent covering over the cockpit of some airplanes.

compress – to squeeze, or press, something closer together to make it fit into a space smaller than it normally takes up.

deflect – to make something change course, or deviate, from its normal path or a straight direction.

deploy – to spread out, extend, or put something into use.

drag – a force that slows down, holds back, or resists the movement of something in the direction intended.

envelope – the fabric part of a balloon or airship that holds the hot air.

fossilize – to rigidly fix and preserve something in Earth's crust; to make something become a fossil.

friction – the force created between two things in contact with each other that makes movement between them harder to accomplish.

gravity – the natural force that pulls all things toward the center of the earth.

hover – to hang in midair, over a certain point or area on the ground below, without flying forward, backward, sideways, or around in circles.

lift – a force pushing upward, such as the upward push created when an airfoil, or wing, moves through the air.

maneuver – to move something in a controlled and skillful way.

migrate – to travel from one location to another to find more suitable living conditions.

pitch – the upward (climb) or downward (dive) movement of an aircraft.

projectile – something hurled, or thrown, through the air that cannot stay in the air on its own.

propulsion – a natural or mechanical force that propels or drives something forward.

prototype – an original pattern, model, or example created to show the form that other objects of that type will take.

reconnaissance – exploration or observation of a specific area or territory to obtain introductory information.

relay – to pass on or transmit items or information in stages, especially over great distances.

rotor blades – horizontal revolving, or rotating, airfoils that provide the lift for aircraft, such as helicopters.

supersonic – able to travel through the air faster than sound waves.

tether – a line, such as a string or a rope, attached to an object to limit its range of movement.

thermals – rising currents of warm air.

throttle – a valve that controls the amount of fuel going to an engine to increase or decrease engine power or thrust.

thrust – a force that pushes or drives something forward, such as from the rotation of a propeller or the pressure of burning fuel from a jet engine.

turbine – the part of an engine that turns, or rotates, to produce power when a steady flow of air, water, steam, or gases pushes against the blades of a rotor.

turbofan engine – a jet engine that produces thrust when a very large fan in the front of the engine pulls air inside to combine with hot exhaust gases leaving the back of the engine.

turbojet engine – a jet engine that produces thrust when

compressed air combines with burning fuel in a combustion chamber and blasts out a jet of high-pressure hot gases.

turboprop engine – a jet engine that produces most of its thrust by means of a turbine-driven propeller.

turboshaft engine – a jet engine similar to a turboprop engine, except, instead of the turbine driving propellers, it powers rotors, like those on a helicopter.

ultralight – a hang glider with an engine-driven propeller.

upthrust – the upward push of cold air against rising warm air or an object that is lighter than air.

yaw – the side-to-side, left and right, turning movement of an aircraft.

BOOKS

Balloon Science. Etta Kaner (Addison–Wesley)

Bats: Ultrasonic Navigators. Secrets of the Animal World (series). Isidro Sanchez (Gareth Stevens)

Cutaway Planes. Clive Gifford (EDC)

The First Supersonic Flight: Captain Charles E. Yaeger Breaks the Sound Barrier. Richard L. Taylor (Watts)

Flight: Fliers and Flying Machines. David Jefferis (Watts)

Hang Gliding. Bob Italia (Abdo and Daughters)

Helicopters. How It Goes (series). Kate Scarborough (Barron)

Kites. Susan Wardle (Price Stern Sloan)

Planes, Gliders, Helicopters, and Other Flying Machines. How Things Work (series). Terry Jennings (LKC)

Rocket! How a Toy Launched the Space Age. Richard Maurer (Crown Books for Young Readers)

Ships of the Air. Lynn Curlee (Houghton Mifflin)

Space and Aircraft. New Technology (series). Nigel Hawkes (TFC Books)

Strange and Wonderful Aircraft. Harvey Weiss (Houghton Mifflin)

VIDEOS

The Big Plane Trip. (Tapeworm Video Distributors)

Come Fly With Us. (Paragon Home Video)

Flying Animals: Winging It. (GPN)

Three Men and a Balloon. (Fast Forward)

The Wright Brothers: How They Invented the Airplane. (SRA School Group)

WEB SITES

muttley.ucdavis.edu/Book/Nature/instructor/gliding-01.html

muttley.ucdavis.edu/Book/Nature/instructor/true-01.html

Some web sites stay current longer than others. For further web sites, use your search engines to locate the following topics: *aircraft, airplanes, flight, flying animals, helicopters, jets, rockets,* and *wings.*

INDEX